_____

from

_____

date

_____

101 inspirational thoughts to BRIGHTEN your DAY

Artwork by
lori Siebert

HARVEST HOUSE PUBLISHERS
EUGENE, OREGON

101 inspirational thoughts to brighten your day

Text Copyright © 2009 by Harvest House Publishers
Art Copyright by Lori Siebert
Published by Harvest House Publishers
Eugene, Oregon 97402
www.harvesthousepublishers.com

ISBN 978-0-7369-2431-3

All works of art reproduced in this book are copyrighted by Lori Siebert and may not be reproduced without the artist's permission. For more information regarding art prints featured in this book, please contact:

Courtney Davis, Inc.
340 Main Street
Franklin, Tennessee 37064

www.courtneydavis.com

Design and production by Garborg Design Works, Savage, Minnesota

Scripture quotations are taken from the HOLY BIBLE, NEW INTERNATIONAL VERSION®. NIV®. Copyright©1973, 1978, 1984 by the International Bible Society. Used by permission of Zondervan. All rights reserved.

Harvest House Publishers has made every effort to trace the ownership of all poems and quotes. In the event of a question arising from the use of a poem or quote, we regret any error made and will be pleased to make the necessary correction in future editions of this book.

Printed in China

11 12 13 14 15 16 / LP / 10 9 8 7 6 5 4 3

happiness resides not in
possessions and not in gold;
the feeling of happiness
dwells in the soul.

DEMOCRITUS

1

happiness
is a habit—
cultivate it.

ELBERT HUBBARD

2

Grab a glass of lemonade and curl up in a comfy chair. Now you're ready to look at some photographs. Enjoy the memories stirred up by images from the summer spent with cousins when you were twelve or the photos that prove you ran a marathon or went bungee jumping. Select some favorite pics and display them near your mirror, desk, front door, or wherever you'll be sure to encounter them each day.

3 hold a true friend with both your hands.

NIGERIAN PROVERB

4 *Let all who take refuge in you be glad; let them ever sing for joy. Spread your protection over them, that those who love your name may rejoice in you.*

THE BOOK OF PSALMS

5

Illusory joy is often worth more than genuine sorrow.

RENE DESCARTES

6

The best way to secure future happiness is to be as happy as is rightfully possible today.

CHARLES W. ELIOT

7

May you
live all the
days of your life.

JONATHAN SWIFT

8

*Happiness depends
on what happens;
Joy does not.*

OSWALD CHAMBERS

9 scatter joy.

RALPH WALDO EMERSON

10

Close the blinds. Turn up the music. And do a few spins around your living room. Don't forget how freeing it is to twirl and stretch and move to soul, rock, classical, inspirational, or Latin music.

11 Take the first step in faith. You don't have to see the whole staircase, just take the first step.

MARTIN LUTHER KING JR.

12 Let me never be afraid of endings or beginnings. Teach me to embrace all of life with joy.

HELEN LESMAN

13 a cheerful look brings joy to the heart,

14

I try to avoid looking forward or backward, and try to keep looking upward.

CHARLOTTE BRONTE

and good news gives health to the bones.

THE BOOK OF PROVERBS

The birds are singing;

15

I don't know what your destiny
will be, but one thing I do know:
the only ones among you who will
be really happy are those who have
sought and found how to serve.

ALBERT SCHWEITZER

16

keep your face always
toward the sunshine—and
shadows will fall behind you.

WALT WHITMAN

17

The Lord your God will bless you in all
your harvest and in all the work of your hands,
and your joy will be complete.

THE BOOK OF DEUTERONOMY

18

As long as there is a chance
of the world getting through
its troubles, I hold that a
reasonable man must behave
as though he were sure of it.
If at the end your cheerfulness
was not justified, at any rate
you will have been cheerful.

WILLIAM SHAKESPEARE

19

*When you have once seen
the glow of happiness on
the face of a beloved person,
you know that a man can
have no vocation but to
awaken that light on the
faces surrounding him; and
you are torn by the thought
of the unhappiness and
night you cast, by the mere
fact of living, in the hearts
you encounter.*

ALBERT CAMUS

20

Take time to read from a great book. Even if there is nobody around to hear you, read portions out loud. Write down quotes that stir your spirit. And celebrate the power of words to infuse your spirit with delight.

21 he sees God's face

22

Joy has nothing to do with material things, or with a man's outward circumstances...A man living in the lap of luxury can be wretched, and a man in the depths of poverty can overflow with joy.

WILLIAM BARCLAY

and shouts for joy.

THE BOOK OF JOB

23

One is happy as a result
of one's own efforts,
once one knows the
necessary ingredients
of happiness—simple
tastes, a certain degree
of courage, self-denial
to a point, love of work,
and, above all, a clear
conscience. Happiness is
no vague dream, of that
I now feel certain.

GEORGE SAND

BUTTERFLIES

The flowers are growing.

24

Always look at what you have left. Never look at what you have lost.

ROBERT H. SCHULLER

25

plant a seed of friendship; reap a bouquet of happiness.

LOIS L. KAUFMAN

26

He is the word that speaks to us in the silences of the hills, and on the plains, and by the rivers. To listen is to be refreshed— is strength and peace.

THE OUTLOOK MAGAZINE, 1901

27

Take time to play with your dog or cat. It delights them and is a great stress-reducer for you. If you don't have a pet, visit the local animal shelter and scratch a few heads or shake a few paws to spread some joy to deserving furry friends.

28

the truest
greatness lies
in being kind,
the truest wisdom
in a happy mind.

ELLA WHEELER WILCOX

29

We see the world not as it is, but rather as we are.

Johann Wolfgang von Goethe

30 no winter lasts
no spring skips

31

Ask and you will receive, and your joy will be complete.

THE BOOK OF JOHN

32

When life becomes overwhelming, head for the backyard or a local park, slip off your shoes, and walk around barefoot on the grass. It's a forgotten joy of childhood that deserves to be revisited!

forever; its turn.

HAL BORLAND

33

Real joy comes not
from ease or riches
or from the praise
of men, but from
doing something
worthwhile.

WILFRED GRENFELL

34

If the world's a vale of tears,
Smile, till rainbows span it!

LUCY LARCOM

35

light tomorrow with today.

ELIZABETH BARRETT BROWNING

36

Don't judge each day by the harvest you reap, but by the seeds you plant.

ROBERT LOUIS STEVENSON

37

Be glad of life, because it gives you the chance to live and to work and to play and to look up at the stars.

HENRY VAN DYKE

38

the joy of the LORD is your strength.

THE BOOK OF NEHEMIAH

39

Start that gratitude journal once and for all. Devote a few minutes each morning or evening to expressing your gratefulness for the daily wonders that make your life rich, vibrant, and full.

40

Happiness is the legal tender of the soul.

ROBERT G. INGERSOLL

strong convictions

The foolish man
seeks happiness in
the distance;
The wise grows it
under his feet.

JAMES OPPENHEIM

42

precede great actions.

LOUISA MAY ALCOTT

43

The essence of optimism is that it takes no account of the present, but it is a source of inspiration, of vitality and hope where others have resigned; it enables a man to hold his head high, to claim the future for himself and not to abandon it to his enemy.

DIETRICH BONHOEFFER

44

You have made known to me the path of life;
you will fill me with joy in your presence.

THE BOOK OF PSALMS

45

those who bring sunshine to
the lives of others cannot keep
it from themselves.

JAMES MATTHEW BARRIE

BUTTERFLIES

The flowers are growing.

*What sunshine is
to flowers, smiles
are to humanity.
These are but
trifles, to be sure;
but scattered
along life's
pathway, the
good they do is
inconceivable.*

JOSEPH ADDISON

47

No matter the season, plan a pick-me-up Saturday morning. Make a nice, big mug of hot cocoa complete with whipped cream and a peppermint stick. Grab the morning paper and curl up in a favorite chair. Revive sweetness in your life.

48

He will yet fill your mouth with laughter and your lips with shouts of joy.

THE BOOK OF JOB

*We have been
friends together
in sunshine and
in shade.*

CAROLINE NORTON

50

in the middle of a
difficulty lies opportunity.

ALBERT EINSTEIN

51

Just living is not enough. One must have sunshine, freedom, and a little flower.

HANS CHRISTIAN ANDERSEN

52

friends are the sunshine of life. JOHN HAY

53

Add a splash of
color to your life.
Select a bouquet
of wildflowers from
your yard or the local
flower market in cheerful
colors. For more lasting
effects, paint a room or
add throw pillows to your
bedroom or living room in
dazzling shades of purple,
aqua, or crimson. The
choices are endless.

54

In everyone's life, at some time, our inner fire goes out. It is then burst into flame by an encounter with another human being. We should all be thankful for those people who rekindle the inner spirit.

ALBERT SCHWEITZER

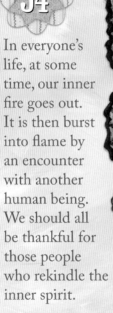

55

*Health is the condition of wisdom, and the sign
is cheerfulness—an open and noble temper.*

RALPH WALDO EMERSON

56

a good laugh is
sunshine in a house.

WILLIAM MAKEPEACE THACKERAY

57

*Nothing but heaven itself
is better than a friend
who is really a friend.*

PLAUTUS

58

my heart leaps for joy and I

59

Let us be grateful to people who make us happy. They are the charming gardeners who make our souls blossom.

MARCEL PROUST

60

Shared joy is a double joy; shared sorrow is half a sorrow.

SWEDISH PROVERB

will give thanks to Him in song.

THE BOOK OF PSALMS

61

A few raindrops changing your plans? Buy a colorful umbrella, raincoat, or pair of red boots. Let every cloud be an opportunity to express yourself in a new way.

62

the sweetest joys a heart can hold grow up between its crosses.

Nixon Waterman

63

Celebrate a milestone
you've reached recently.
Reward yourself with
an afternoon matinee
or a manicure or an
evening with friends.
Honor your journey by
acknowledging the big
and small achievements!

64

Perfume and incense bring joy to
the heart, and the pleasantness of one's
friend springs from his earnest counsel.

THE BOOK OF PROVERBS

65

the less of routine,
the more of life.

AMOS BRONSON ALCOTT

66

You don't have a soul.
You are a soul. You have a body.

C.S. LEWIS

67

To live content with small means;
to seek elegance rather than luxury,
and refinement rather than fashion;
to be worthy, not respectable, and
wealthy, not rich; to study hard, think
quietly, talk frankly; to listen to stars
and birds, to babes and sages, with
an open heart; to bear all cheerfully,
do all bravely, await occasion, hurry
never; in a word, to let the spiritual,
unbidden and unconscious, grow up
through the common: this is to be
my symphony.

WILLIAM HENRY CHANNING

it is good to lengthen
to the last a sunny mood.

JAMES RUSSELL LOWELL

69

The trees of the forest will sing, they will sing for joy before the Lord.

THE BOOK OF FIRST CHRONICLES

70

only a life lived for others
is a life worthwhile.

ALBERT EINSTEIN

71

There is one friend in the life of each
of us who seems not a separate person,
however dear and beloved, but an
expansion, an interpretation, of one's
self, the very meaning of one's soul.

EDITH WHARTON

72

Enjoy your town with a fresh perspective. Check out the visitor's info for your area and select activities or restaurants that you've never considered. Grab a friend or two and hit the town with all of the wonder and joy of a tourist.

73

Remember, we all stumble, every one of us. That's why it's a comfort to go hand in hand.

EMILY KIMBROUGH

74

Do you have neighbors you've never met? Make the effort to say hello to someone who lives near you. Develop connections with others, and you'll weave a web of support, friendship, and strength.

75

the best way to cheer yourself up is to try to cheer somebody else up.

MARK TWAIN

76

A cheerful temper joined with innocence will make beauty attractive, knowledge delightful, and wit good-natured.

JOSEPH ADDISON

77

Those who sow in tears will reap with songs of joy.

THE BOOK OF PSALMS

78

You find yourself refreshed by the presence of cheerful people. Why not make an honest effort to confer that pleasure on others? Half the battle is gained if you never allow yourself to say anything gloomy.

Lydia M. Child

79

life's a voyage that's homeward bound.

Herman Melville

whoever is happy will

Take a box of note cards and a favorite pen along with you to a local coffee shop. Enjoy your drink of choice and spend an hour sharing about your life and encouraging friends or family members you rarely see.

make others happy too.

82

The laughter of man is the contentment of God.

JOHN WEISS

Happiness lies in the joy of achievement and the thrill of creative effort.

FRANKLIN DELANO ROOSEVELT

83

84

Each morning sees some task begin,
Each evening sees it close;
Something attempted, something done,
Has earned a night's repose.

HENRY WADSWORTH LONGFELLOW

85

go for a walk today and
of life and joy. listen to

86

Wondrous is the strength of cheerfulness, and its power of endurance—the cheerful man will do more in the same time; will do it better, will preserve it longer, than the sad or sullen.

THOMAS CARLYLE

pay attention to all the sounds
the symphony of being alive.

87

Is it so small a thing
To have enjoyed the sun,
To have lived light in the spring,
To have loved, to have thought, to have done.

MATTHEW ARNOLD

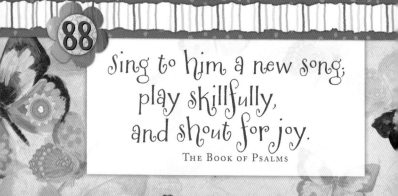

88

sing to him a new song;
play skillfully,
and shout for joy.

THE BOOK OF PSALMS

89

I count this thing to be grandly true: That a noble deed is a step toward God.

JOSIAH G. HOLLAND

90

The cheerful live longest in years, and afterward in our regards. Cheerfulness is the off-shoot of goodness.

CHRISTIAN NESTELL BOVEE

91

the soul of sweet delight
can never be defiled.

WILLIAM BLAKE

92

Sunshine is delicious, rain is refreshing,
wind braces us up, snow is exhilarating;
there is really no such thing as bad weather,
only different kinds of good weather.

JOHN RUSKIN

93

All who win joy must share it;
happiness was born a twin.

LORD BYRON

94

*Far away there in the
sunshine are my highest
aspirations. I may not
reach them but I can
look up and see their
beauty, believe in them
and try to follow them.*

LOUISA MAY ALCOTT

95

we turn not older
with years but
newer every day.

EMILY DICKINSON

96

A man finds joy in giving an apt

97

When the thought of a friend makes you laugh and gives you joy, take time to jot a postcard to her, send her an email, or give her a call and let her know she makes you smile.

98

No pessimist ever discovered the secrets of the stars, or sailed to an uncharted land, or opened a new heaven to the human spirit.

HELEN KELLER

reply—and how good is a timely word!

THE BOOK OF PROVERBS

99

goodness is a special
kind of truth
and beauty. it is
truth and beauty
in human behavior.

HARRY ALLEN OVERSTREET

100

If instead of a gem, or even a flower, we should cast the gift of a loving thought into the heart of a friend, that would be giving as the angels give.

George MacDonald

101

Add light to your day and bring cheer to those you encounter by offering a smile, a kind word, a moment of laughter, or a gesture of help and hope. Make a difference today and brighten the world!

scripture references